Spelling and Decoding

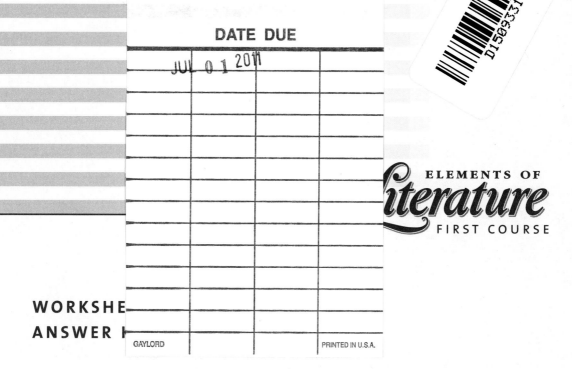

DATE DUE

JUL 0 1 2011

GAYLORD · PRINTED IN U.S.A.

WORKSHE

ANSWER K

ELEMENTS OF
Literature
FIRST COURSE

HOLT, RINEHART AND WINSTON
Harcourt Brace & Company

Austin • New York • Orlando • Atlanta • San Francisco • Boston • Dallas • Toronto • London

Staff Credits

Associate Director: Mescal Evler

Manager of Editorial Operations: Robert R. Hoyt

Managing Editor: Bill Wahlgren

Project Editor: Katie Vignery

Component Editor: Scott Hall

Editorial Staff: *Associate Editors,* Kathryn Rogers, Christopher LeCluyse; *Assistant Managing Editor,* Mandy Beard; *Copyediting Supervisor,* Michael Neibergall; *Senior Copyeditor,* Mary Malone; *Copyeditors,* Joel Bourgeois, Jeffrey T. Holt, Suzi A. Hunn, Jane Kominek, Désirée Reid; *Editorial Coordinators,* Marie H. Price, Robert Littlefield, Mark Holland, Jill Chertudi, Marcus Johnson, Tracy DeMont; *Support Staff,* Pat Stover, Matthew Villalobos; *Word Processors,* Ruth Hooker, Margaret Sanchez, Kelly Kelley, Elizabeth Butler

Permissions: Tamara A. Blanken, Ann B. Farrar

Design: *Art Director, Book Design,* Richard Metzger; *Design Manager, Book & Media Design,* Joe Melomo

Prepress Production: Beth Prevelige, Simira Davis, Sergio Durante

Manufacturing Coordinator: Michael Roche

ISBN 0-03-052463-6

7 8 9 10 11 022 06 05 04 03 02

TABLE OF CONTENTS

TO THE TEACHER vi

COLLECTION ONE:
OUT HERE ON MY OWN

Rikki-tikki-tavi • *Rudyard Kipling*
Spelling Worksheet: Spelling Words With the Endings *-er / -est* .. 1

Song of the Trees • *Mildred D. Taylor*
Spelling Worksheet: Spelling Adverbs 2

The Smallest Dragonboy • *Anne McCaffrey*
Spelling Worksheet: Spelling Words with Adjective- and
Noun-Forming Suffixes 3

Three Skeleton Key • *George G. Toudouze*
Spelling Worksheet: Spelling Compound Words 4

A Day's Wait • *Ernest Hemingway*
Decoding Worksheet: Mind Those *p*'s 5

COLLECTION TWO:
WHO AM I?

from **Homesick** • *Jean Fritz*
Spelling Worksheet: Spelling Words Containing
Consonant Blends 6

from **Barrio Boy** • *Ernesto Galarza*
Spelling Worksheet: Spelling School Words 7

Fish Cheeks • *Amy Tan*
Spelling Worksheet: Spelling Words from the Kitchen 8

Names/Nombres • *Julia Alvarez*
Decoding Worksheet: Verbs to Nouns 9

The Naming of Names • *Ray Bradbury*
Spelling Worksheet: Spelling Words Formed from Word Roots
and Base Words 10

COLLECTION THREE:
DO THE RIGHT THING

After Twenty Years • *O. Henry*
Decoding Worksheet: The Letters *c* and *g* 11

A Mason-Dixon Memory • *Clifton Davis*
Spelling Worksheet: Spelling Regular and Irregular Plurals 12

The No-Guitar Blues • *Gary Soto*
Spelling Worksheet: How to Own a Word: Words with *ie* and *ei*
Irregular Spelling Words 13

Bargain • *A. B. Guthrie*
Spelling Worksheet: How to Own a Word: Silent Letters
Spelling Words from the Nineteenth-Century West 14

Amigo Brothers • *Piri Thomas*
Spelling Worksheet: Spelling Words Containing
Double Consonants 15

COLLECTION FOUR:
WE ROOKIES HAVE TO STICK TOGETHER

Brian's Song • *William Blinn*
Spelling Worksheet: Spelling Football Words 16

COLLECTION FIVE:
LIVING IN THE HEART

User Friendly • *T. Ernesto Bethancourt*
Decoding Worksheet: Long and Short Vowel Sounds 17

Miss Awful • *Arthur Cavanaugh*
Spelling Worksheet: Spelling Homonyms 18

COLLECTION SIX:
THIS OLD EARTH

Sky Woman • *retold by Joseph Bruchac*
Spelling Worksheet: How to Own a Word: Adding
Suffixes: Change *y* to *i*
Adding Suffixes to Words that End in *y* 19

When the Earth Shakes • *Patricia Lauber*
Spelling Worksheet: Spelling Vivid Verbs 20

from **Survive the Savage Sea** • *Dougal Robertson*
Decoding Worksheet: Consonant Combinations 21

Antaeus • *Borden Deal*
Spelling Worksheet: Spelling Contractions Correctly 22

COLLECTION SEVEN:
OUR CLASSICAL HERITAGE

The Origin of the Seasons • *retold by Olivia Coolidge*
Spelling Worksheet: How to Own a Word: Prefixes
Spelling Words from Mythology 23

Orpheus, the Great Musician • *retold by Olivia Coolidge*
Spelling Worksheet: Spelling Words Containing Inflected
Endings *-s, -ed, -ing* 24

Echo and Narcissus • *retold by Roger Lancelyn Green*
Decoding Worksheet: Reading Greek Words 25

The Labors of Hercules • *retold by Rex Warner*
Spelling Worksheet: Spelling Words That Are Often Misspelled . . 26

COLLECTION EIGHT:
900 CINDERELLAS:
OUR WORLD HERITAGE IN FOLKLORE

Aschenputtel • *retold by Jakob and Wilhelm Grimm*
Decoding Worksheet: Spelling Words with Germanic Roots 27

The Algonquin Cinderella • *retold by M. R. Cox*
Yeh-Shen • *retold by Ai-Ling Louie*
Spelling Worksheet: How to Own a Word: Doubling
Consonants Before Suffixes
Spelling Words Ending in *e* and *y* 28

Oni and the Great Bird • *retold by Abayomi Fuja*
Spelling Worksheet: Words with *ie* 29

Master Frog • *retold by Lynette Dyer Vuong*
Spelling Worksheet: Spelling Multisyllabic Words 30

Sealskin, Soulskin • *retold by Clarissa Pinkola Estés*
Spelling Worksheet: Spelling Inuit Words and
Words of the Far North 31

ANSWER KEY 33

The copying masters in this *Spelling and Decoding* booklet have been organized by collection; within the collections, worksheets are arranged by selection. Spelling Worksheets present students with lists of spelling words from the selections. The spelling words have been identified based on their level of difficulty and are grouped according to shared structural characteristics or subject matter. Decoding Worksheets explore letter-sound correspondences and word structure patterns represented in the vocabulary of the selection. Decoding strategies have been determined based on their relevance to the words in the selection, as well as their general utility and grade-level appropriateness.

The activity formats of the worksheets are varied to maintain high interest. Some activities, for instance, encourage students to focus on what words look like; others require students to use the words within the context of writing or revising activities; while still others guide students in analyzing word structure to understand both spelling and meaning. In addition to these activity formats, some Spelling Worksheets provide additional practice based on the How to Own a Word feature that follows the selections.

ANSWER KEY

The Answer Key provides answers to all exercises in this booklet.

SPELLING WORKSHEET

Rikki-tikki-tavi
Rudyard Kipling   **Pupil's Edition page 2**

Spelling Words With the Endings *–er/–est*

In making comparisons, adjectives and adverbs take special forms. The form that is used depends on how many things are being compared. Follow these rules when forming the different degrees of comparison.

1. Most one-syllable modifiers form their comparative and superlative degrees by adding *-er* and *-est*. For example, *near* becomes *nearer* and *nearest.*
   NOTE: Words ending with *–y* change *y* to *i* before adding *-er* or *-est*. For example, *dry* becomes *drier* and *driest.*

2. Some two-syllable modifiers form their comparative and superlative degrees by adding *-er* and *-est*. Other two-syllable modifiers form their comparative and superlative degrees by using *more* and *most*. For example, *careful* becomes *more careful* and *most careful.*
   NOTE: Words ending with *–y* change *y* to *i* before adding *-er* or *-est*. For example, *lonely* becomes *lonelier* and *loneliest.*

3. Modifiers that have three or more syllables form their comparative and superlative degrees by using *more* and *most*. For example, dangerous becomes *more dangerous* and *most dangerous.*

Below is a list of some modifiers found in "Rikki-tikki-tavi."

angry	careful	early	faint	near
safe	soon	wise	dangerous	sorrowfully

EXERCISE A

On the lines provided, write the forms of the spelling word above that match each description.

1. the superlative form of *careful*   _____

2. the comparative form of *dangerous* _____

3. the comparative form of *angry*   _____

4. the superlative form of *sorrowfully* _____

5. the superlative form of *near*   _____

EXERCISE B

On the lines provided, write the appropriate forms of each word in parentheses.

1. Of the six people in my family, Mother is usually the _____ riser. (*early*)

2. The baby bird is _____ in the nest than he is on the ground. (*safe*)

3. He is _____ than Darzee. (*wise*)

4. It was a battle that came _____ than expected. (*soon*)

5. The baby bird's cry is the _____ sound of all. (*faint*)

Elements of Literature   *Spelling and Decoding Worksheets* **1**

SPELLING WORKSHEET

Song of the Trees
Mildred D. Taylor   **Pupil's Edition page 28**

Spelling Adverbs

Adverbs are words that tell *how, when, where, why, how much,* and *to what extent*. As you'll see in the following list of words from "Song of the Trees," not all adverbs end in *-ly.* For those adverbs that are formed by adding suffixes such as *-ly,* there are a few special spelling rules to remember.

1. When adding the suffix *-ly* to a word, the spelling of the word usually remains the same. The exception to this rule is words that end in *y*. For most words that end in *y,* change the *y* to *i* before adding *-ly.* For example, *day + ly* becomes *daily.*

2. When adding other adverb-forming suffixes, such as *-ward,* the spelling of the word generally does not change.

Now, get ready to practice spelling these helpful descriptive words.

afterward	down	incredulously
already	enough	later
away	gently	nearby
comfortably	haughtily	softly
curtly	here	suspiciously

EXERCISE A

On the lines provided, write the spelling words that match each description.

1. the adverb with five syllables: _____

2. the adverb in which the sound /sh/ is spelled *ci:* _____

3. the vowel combination *ea* is pronounced differently in each of these

    two adverbs: _____ , _____

4. the two adverbs with the consonant combination *rt:* _____ ,

    _____

5. the one-syllable adverb pronounced *hēr:* _____

EXERCISE B

On the lines provided, write the adverbs listed above that contain the same letters as the corresponding smaller words.

1. ear _____   6. ward _____

2. own _____   7. no _____

3. fort _____   8. way _____

4. aught _____   9. soft _____

5. gent _____   10. ate _____

Elements of Literature

SPELLING WORKSHEET

The Smallest Dragonboy
Anne McCaffrey   **Pupil's Edition page 46**

Spelling Words with Adjective- and Noun-Forming Suffixes

Adding a suffix to a word changes the way that you can use that word in a sentence. For instance, by adding the suffix *-ful* to the noun *pain,* you create the adjective *painful.* Similarly, you can turn the adjective *obedient* into the noun *obedience* by replacing the suffix *-ent* with the suffix *-ence.* When adding suffixes to words, there are a few special spelling rules to remember.

1. When a suffix begins with a vowel, as *-able* or *-est* does, drop the final silent *e* of the word. For example, *love + able* becomes *lovable.* However, when the word ends in *ce* or *ge,* as *notice* or *courage* does, and the suffix begins with *a* or *o,* as *-able* or *-ous* does, the suffix is simply added to the word without changing the spelling. For example, *courage + ous* becomes *courageous.*

2. When a suffix begins with a consonant, as *-less* or *-ful* does, the spelling of the base word usually remains the same, even if it ends in *e.* For example, *care + less* becomes *careless.* There are a few exceptions to this rule, like the word *true,* which becomes *truly.*

3. For words that end in *-y* preceded by a consonant, as in the word *friendly,* change the *y* to *i* before adding any suffix that does not begin with an *i,* like *-er* or *-ful* or *-ous.* For example, *friendly + er* becomes *friendlier.*

Study these words from "The Smallest Dragonboy."

argument	flexible	harmless	resentful	traditional
constriction	glorious	opportunity	swiftness	unmistakable

EXERCISE A

On the lines provided, write the form of each word required in the following sentences.

1. The suffix *-ous* changes the noun *glory* to the adjective _____.

2. The suffix *-ion* changes the verb *constrict* to the noun _____.

3. The suffix *-ful* changes the verb *resent* to the adjective _____.

4. The suffix *-al* changes the noun *tradition* to the adjective _____.

5. The suffix *-ity* changes the adjective *opportune* to the noun _____.

EXERCISE B

On the lines provided, write the missing letters that complete each of the following spelling words.

1. _____ unity

2. _____ gum _____

3. _____ sent _____

4. _____ if _____

5. _____ strict _____

6. flex _____

7. _____ mist _____

8. _____ arm _____

SPELLING WORKSHEET

Three Skeleton Key
George G. Toudouze   **Pupil's Edition page 64**

Spelling Compound Words

Compound words are made by joining two words so they function as one. *Sidewalk,* for instance, is a compound word because it is a combination of *side* and *walk.* Most compounds are closed words like *sidewalk.* Compounds like *police officer* are open, which means that even though the two words are separate, they are thought of as one. Other compounds are hyphenated, as *half-moon* is. Practice spelling these compounds from "Three Skeleton Key."

coast guard	metalwork	sundown
footfall	nightfall	twenty-four
glassed-in	old-timers	well-placed
knee-deep	patrol boat	windmill
lighthouse	stronghold	no one

EXERCISE A

On the lines provided, write each spelling word in the column to which it belongs.

Open Compounds   **Hyphenated Compounds**   **Closed Compounds**

1. _____   4. _____   9. _____

2. _____   5. _____   10. _____

3. _____   6. _____   11. _____

                         7. _____   12. _____

                         8. _____   13. _____

                                                   14. _____

                                                   15. _____

EXERCISE B

On the lines provided, add the missing consonants that complete each of the following spelling words.

1. __ a __ __ o __   __ oa __

2. __ __ a __ __ e __ -i __

3. __ oo __ __ a __ __

4. __ i __ __ __ i __ __

5. __ e __ a __ __ o __ __

6. __ i __ __ __ __ ou __ e

7. __ u __ __ o __ __

8. __ __ __ e __ __ y- __ ou __

9. __ i __ __ __ __ a __ __

10. __ __ ee- __ ee __

11. __ o o __ e

12. __ __ a __ __   __ u __ __ __

13. o __ __ - __ i __ e __ __

14. __ e __ __ - __ __ a __ e

15. __ __ __ o __ __ __ o __ __

DECODING WORKSHEET

A Day's Wait
Ernest Hemingway   **Pupil's Edition page 80**

Mind Those *p*'s

Many words that come from Greek have unexpected *p*'s—*p*'s that are silent and *p*'s that stand for sounds other than /p/. In English words borrowed from Greek, *p* is usually silent before *n*, *t*, and *s* when both letters are in the same syllable. When *p* is combined with *h* in the same syllable, the two letters together stand for the sound /f/.

EXERCISE A

Each of these pairs of words contains *p* followed by another consonant. In one of the words, the *p* is silent. Circle each word that has a silent *p*. Then, use the circled words to complete the sentences.

	pt		**ps**		**pn**		**ps**		**pt**
1.	optimistic	**2.**	psychology	**3.**	hypnotic	**4.**	pseudonym	**5.**	helicopter
	ptomaine		capsize		pneumonia		eclipse		pterodactyl

6. A _____ is a flying reptile that lived during the time of the dinosaurs.

7. Training a dog requires understanding something about the dog's _____ .

8. Every day in the mess hall, the campers made jokes about getting _____ poisoning.

9. The author uses a _____ rather than her real name.

10. _____ is a disease that afflicts the lungs.

EXERCISE B

Each of these pairs of words contains the letter combination *ph*. Read the words, and circle the ones in which *ph* stands for the sound /f/. Then, use the circled words to complete the sentences.

	1.	shepherd		**2.**	graphic		**3.**	upholstery	**4.**	phantom		**5.**	physician
		emphasis			upheaval			phonics		haphazard			loophole

6. You put more _____ on the accented syllable than on the unaccented syllable.

7. They called him the _____ gardener because no one ever saw him actually working.

8. One method of teaching spelling and reading rules is called _____ .

9. The poster was designed by a _____ artist.

10. The _____ advised the patient to get more rest and improve her diet.

Elements of Literature   *Spelling and Decoding Worksheets* **5**

SPELLING WORKSHEET

from Homesick
Jean Fritz   Pupil's Edition page 104

Spelling Words Containing Consonant Blends

Consonant blends are groups of consecutive letters that work together to form word sounds. Most blends are two-letter groups like *br, ck, pl,* and *sn.* However, there are also three-letter blends like *str* and *tch.* Review these words from "Homesick," and identify the blends in each word. Some of the blends will be at the beginning of the word; others will be hidden in the middle; some will fall at the end.

broad-brimmed	crooked	freedom	interest	probably
classes	dreamed	glowering	o'clock	straight
clutched	flustered	gradually	please	truly

EXERCISE A

Study these patterns of tall letters, small letters, and letters that go below the line. In the boxes provided, write the spelling word whose letters match each shape.

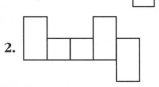

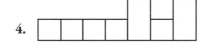

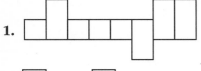

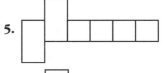

EXERCISE B

On the lines provided, write the spelling words that match each pronunciation.

1. graˊjo͞o•əl•lē _____

2. klucht _____

3. frēˊdəm _____

4. brôd-brimd _____

5. tro͞oˊlē _____

6. flusˊtərd _____

7. strāt _____

8. glouˊər•iŋ _____

9. präbˊə•blē _____

10. ə•kläkˊ _____

EXERCISE C

On the lines provided, write the spelling words that contain the same letters as the corresponding smaller words.

1. lease _____

2. luster _____

3. rest _____

4. dual _____

5. road _____

6. lower _____

7. rook _____

8. reed _____

9. rob _____

10. lass _____

6 *Spelling and Decoding Worksheets*   *Elements of Literature*

SPELLING WORKSHEET

from Barrio Boy
Ernesto Galarza

Pupil's Edition page 124

Spelling School Words

These words from "Barrio Boy" all relate to the experiences of a boy spending his first day in a new school. You've probably heard most of these words before. Now it's time to learn how to spell them.

announcements	consultations	friendliness	knowledge	progress
attention	enrolling	graduated	patiently	pronounce
blackboard	formidable	interpreter	principal	recitations

EXERCISE A

On the lines provided, write the correct spellings of each word.

1. pashently _____

2. atention _____

3. blackbord _____

4. principel _____

5. knowlege _____

6. resitations _____

7. interprator _____

8. inroling _____

9. anouncmints _____

10. friendlynes _____

EXERCISE B

On the lines provided, write the word or words that match each description.

1. the five words that contain double consonants: _____, _____, _____, _____, _____

2. the four words in which the sound /sh/ is spelled *ti:* _____, _____, _____, _____

3. the two words in which the sound /ow/ is spelled *ou:* _____, _____

4. the five words that contain four syllables: _____, _____, _____, _____, _____

5. the word in which the sound /j/ is spelled *dge:* _____

SPELLING WORKSHEET

Fish Cheeks
Amy Tan Pupil's Edition page 134

Spelling Words from the Kitchen

These words from "Fish Cheeks" name a variety of Chinese and American foods and customs. Don't be fooled even though they seem so simple. Each one offers a particular spelling challenge.

appreciate	custom	platters	cod	tofu
belched	fungus	polite	squid	turkey
chopsticks	menu	prawns	sweet potatoes	veins

EXERCISE A

On the lines provided, write the spelling words that match each pronunciation.

1. käd _____

2. fuŋ′gəs _____

3. pə•līt′ _____

4. ə•prē′shē•āt′ _____

5. tō′fo͞o _____

6. men′yo͞o _____

7. plat′ərz _____

8. skwid _____

9. tʉr′kē _____

10. prônz _____

EXERCISE B

Complete this crossword grid with the correct spelling words.

DECODING WORKSHEET

Names/Nombres
Julia Alvarez **Pupil's Edition page 144**

Verbs to Nouns

When the suffix *-tion, -ion,* or *-ation* is added to a verb, the verb becomes a noun. In addition to changing the way a word is used, adding the suffix *-tion, -ion,* or *-ation* changes the way the word is pronounced. When *-tion, -ion,* or *-ation* is added, the primary stress shifts to the next-to-the-last syllable.

NOTE: Always drop the final *e* before adding a suffix that begins with a vowel. (*locate + ion = location*).

EXERCISE A

Read these pairs of verbs and nouns. Each word appears twice: first as a whole word and then broken into syllables. Circle the syllable that gets the most stress when you say the word.

EXAMPLE:	consider	con (sid) er	consideration	con sid er (a) tion
1.	immigrate	im mi grate	immigration	im mi gra tion
2.	celebrate	cel e brate	celebration	cel e bra tion
3.	distribute	dis trib ute	distribution	dis tri bu tion
4.	explain	ex plain	explanation	ex pla na tion
5.	multiply	mul ti ply	multiplication	mul ti pli ca tion
6.	define	de fine	definition	def i ni tion
7.	participate	par tic i pate	participation	par tic i pa tion
8.	limit	lim it	limitation	lim i ta tion
9.	resign	re sign	resignation	res ig na tion
10.	dictate	dic tate	dictation	dic ta tion

EXERCISE B

The suffix *-tion, -ion,* or *-ation* can be added to each of the following verbs to form nouns. Read the verb, and write the number of syllables you hear. Then, write the noun form of the verb and the number of syllables you hear in the noun.

EXAMPLE:	introduce	_3_	introduction	_4_
1.	communicate	___	_____	___
2.	revise	___	_____	___
3.	declare	___	_____	___
4.	populate	___	_____	___
5.	reserve	___	_____	___

SPELLING WORKSHEET

The Naming of Names
Ray Bradbury   Pupil's Edition page 152

Spelling Words Formed from Word Roots and Base Words

All of the words listed below are combinations of several word parts. Each contains either a base word or a word root. A base word is a complete word and can stand alone. Other word parts, like prefixes and suffixes, can be added to a base word to make new words. For example, *freedom* is made up of the base word *free* plus the suffix *-dom*.

A word root, however, cannot stand alone. The root of a word is the part that carries the word's main meaning. It is always combined with one or more word parts. For example, the root *-ject* means "throw." It is combined with another word part to make the word *reject*, which means "throw back."

The following words are from "The Naming of Names."

Word	Root or Base	Word	Root or Base
altitude	*alt* means "high"	**encyclop**edia	*encyclo* means "circle";
ana**chron**ism	*chron* means "time"		*ped* means "education"
archaeologist	*archaeo* means "ancient";	in**sane**	*sane* means "healthy"
	log means "study of"	per**spire**	*spire* means "breathe"
atmosphere	*atmos* means "vapor";	**philosoph**y	*philo* means "love";
	sphere means "planet"		*soph* means "knowledge"
con**struct**ing	*struct* means "build"	pre**cise**	*cise* means "cut"
con**viv**ial	*viv* means "live" or	**quiet**ly	*quiet* means "still"
	"alive"	**sens**ible	*sens* means "feel"
dis**solve**	*solve* means "loosen"	sub**merge**d	*merge* means "plunge"

EXERCISE A

On the lines provided, write the words that contain each of the following roots or bases.

1. merge _____

2. ped _____

3. sane _____

4. spire _____

5. sphere _____

6. struct _____

7. chron _____

8. philo _____

9. quiet _____

10. sens _____

EXERCISE B

On the lines provided, write the missing vowels that complete the following spelling words.

1. d ___ ss ___ lv ___

2. pr ___ c ___ s ___

3. ___ ns ___ n ___

4. c ___ nv ___ v ___ ___ l

5. s ___ bm ___ rg ___ d

6. c ___ nstr ___ ct ___ ng

7. ___ lt ___ t ___ d ___

8. ___ rch ___ ___ l ___ g ___ st

10 *Spelling and Decoding Worksheets*   *Elements of Literature*

DECODING WORKSHEET

After Twenty Years
O. Henry

Pupil's Edition page 192

The Letters *c* and *g*

The letters *c* and *g* have an unusual distinction in English. They both have a hard sound and a soft sound. Hard *c* sounds like *k* (as in *cottage*), and soft *c* sounds like *s* (as in *center*). Hard *g* is heard in *game* and *good,* and soft *g* sounds like *j* (as in *gentle*). Which sound *c* and *g* have depends on the letters that follow them.

• Both *c* and *g* are usually hard before *a, o,* and *u.*
• Both *c* and *g* are usually soft before *e* and *i.*
• Both *c* and *g* are hard when they are followed by another consonant, as in the blends *cl* and *cr* and *gl* and *gr.*
• Both *c* and *g* are hard when they are the last letter in a word, but they are soft when followed by final *e.*

EXERCISE A

Study these words from "After Twenty Years." Then, write the words that match the descriptions below.

certain	pacific	cigar	compete	distance
correspond	passengers	success	submerged	egotism

1. two words that contain hard *g* _____ _____

2. two words that begin with soft *c* _____ _____

3. two words that begin with hard *c* _____ _____

4. two words that contain both hard *c* and soft *c* _____ _____

5. two words that contain soft *g* _____ _____

EXERCISE B

Write the following words under the correct headings.

existence	panic	swagger	stranger
description	eager	dangerous	announced

Words Containing a Hard *c*

1. _____

2. _____

Words Containing a Soft *c*

3. _____

4. _____

Words Containing a Hard *g*

5. _____

6. _____

Words Containing a Soft *g*

7. _____

8. _____

SPELLING WORKSHEET

A Mason-Dixon Memory
Clifton Davis

Pupil's Edition page 205

Spelling Regular and Irregular Plurals

To form the plural of many English nouns, you need only add an *s*. To form irregular plurals, however, study these guidelines.

- For nouns ending in *s, x, z, ch,* or *sh,* add *es.*
- For nouns ending in *y* preceded by a vowel, add *s.*
- For nouns ending in *y* preceded by a consonant, change *y* to *i* and add *es.*
- For some nouns ending in *f* or *fe,* add *s.* For others, change the *f* or *fe* to *v* and add *es.*
- Some nouns ending in *o* preceded by a consonant form their plurals by adding *es;* some form their plurals by adding *s.*
- The plurals of a few nouns are formed in irregular ways. These must be memorized.

Practice spelling the plurals of the following words from "A Mason-Dixon Memory."

attorneys	businessmen	disasters	friendships	parishes
boundaries	classes	echoes	ladies	speeches
buses	coaches	facilities	lives	statues

EXERCISE A

On the lines provided, write the correct plural forms next to each singular word.

1. box _____

2. knife _____

3. radio _____

4. comedy _____

5. scientist _____

6. monkey _____

7. birch _____

8. photo _____

9. chairwoman _____

10. arrangement _____

11. church _____

12. bush _____

13. dress _____

14. trophy _____

15. theory _____

EXERCISE B

Unscramble the following letters to reveal the spelling words from "A Mason-Dixon Memory" listed above.

1. shape sir _____

2. veils _____

3. he speecs _____

4. a test us _____

5. a bride on us _____

6. stony rate _____

7. sad rest is _____

8. case hoc _____

9. a slide _____

10. red fish spin _____

Elements of Literature

SPELLING WORKSHEET

The No-Guitar Blues

Gary Soto   **Pupil's Edition page 216**

✔ How to Own a Word: Words with *ie* and *ei*

In the following sentences, cross out the italicized words that are spelled incorrectly. Write the correct spelling of the word on the line provided. If the word is already spelled correctly, write **C.**

1. Fausto *seized* the chance to make money when he saw a lost dog. _____

2. He *recieved* a handsome reward from the owners. _____

3. Had he *acheived* the reward dishonestly? _____

4. It was absolutely *eerei* that he felt so guilty. _____

5. Fausto thought the *preist* looked right at him. _____

Irregular Spelling Words

These words from "The No-Guitar Blues" are all exceptions: Not a single one is spelled the way you might expect. Most of them have silent letters. Practice spelling these tricky words.

brighter	earn	license	scratch	through
caught	guitar	perpetual	special	watched
deceitful	heard	pleasant	sweat	weird

EXERCISE A

On the lines provided, write the correct spelling of each word.

1. lisense _____   **6.** thru _____

2. briter _____   **7.** wierd _____

3. plesent _____   **8.** ern _____

4. wacht _____   **9.** deseetful _____

5. swet _____   **10.** speshel _____

EXERCISE B

On the lines provided, write the spelling words listed above that contain the same letters as the corresponding smaller words.

1. plea _____   **6.** eat _____

2. rough _____   **7.** aught _____

3. pet _____   **8.** hear _____

4. right _____   **9.** lice _____

5. rat _____   **10.** tar _____

SPELLING WORKSHEET

Bargain

A. B. Guthrie   Pupil's Edition page 230

✔ **How to Own a Word: Silent Letters**

On the line provided, write the correct spelling of each of the following words. If the word is already spelled correctly, write **C.**

1. climed _____

2. edged _____

3. consined _____

4. hussle _____

5. neumonia _____

Spelling Words from the Nineteenth-Century West

These nouns from the days of the Wild West include several open and closed compounds. Practice spelling the following nouns from "Bargain."

blizzard	buttes	kerosene	moustache	saddle horse
boardwalk	freighter	lantern	overshoes	saloon
buckboard	harness shop	mercantile	pitchfork	whiskey barrel

EXERCISE A

On the lines provided, write the spelling words that match each of the following descriptions.

1. the four words that are closed compounds: _____, _____,

   _____, _____

2. the three words that are open compounds: _____, _____,

   _____

3. the word which contains a double vowel: _____

4. the word which contains a double *z:* _____

5. the one-syllable word: _____

EXERCISE B

On the lines provided, write the missing consonants that complete each of the following spelling words.

1. ____ e ____ ____ a ____ ____ i ____ e

2. ____ a ____ ____ e ____ ____

3. ____ ou ____ ____ a ____ ____ e

4. ____ ____ ei ____ ____ ____ e ____

5. ____ ____ i ____ ____ a ____ ____

SPELLING WORKSHEET

Amigo Brothers
Piri Thomas

Spelling Words Containing Double Consonants

All of the following words from "Amigo Brothers" have double consonants. Some of the consonants are doubled because suffixes have been added; some consonants are doubled because prefixes have been added; and other words simply have double consonants as their base.

announcer	challenger	dispelled	medallion	progress
approval	community	flurry	occasionally	stillness
bragging	corridor	immediately	profession	surrounding

EXERCISE A

On the lines provided, write the spelling words that contain the same letters as the corresponding smaller words.

1. ill _____

2. media _____

3. unity _____

4. hall _____

5. lion _____

6. noun _____

7. rag _____

8. rid _____

9. flu _____

10. round _____

EXERCISE B

On the lines provided, write the correct spelling of each of the following words.

1. flury _____

2. medalion _____

3. proggres _____

4. coriddor _____

5. proffesion _____

6. anouncer _____

7. disspeled _____

8. ocassionaly _____

9. surounding _____

10. aproval _____

EXERCISE C

On the lines provided, complete each analogy with a spelling word.

EXAMPLE: *Ear* is to *hear* as _____*eye*_____ is to *see.*

1. *Started* is to *completed* as _____ is to *gathered.*

2. *House* is to *hallway* as *hospital* is to _____ .

3. _____ is to *award* as *uniform* is to *clothing.*

4. *People* are to _____ as *geese* are to *flock.*

5. *Teaching* is to _____ as *bird-watching* is to *hobby.*

Elements of Literature

SPELLING WORKSHEET

Brian's Song
William Blinn   Pupil's Edition page 273

Spelling Football Words

There would be little action in *Brian's Song* without the words listed below. After all, how can you talk about football players without using the terms of their game? Even if you aren't a football fan, learning to spell these words will improve your everyday spelling. Study these words from *Brian's Song*.

blitz	end zone	kickoff	punt	scrimmage
cleats	fullback	offense	receiver	sportscaster
defense	halfback	quarterback	playbook	touchdown

EXERCISE A

On the lines provided, write the spelling words that match each description.

1. the plural word: _____

2. the open compound word: _____

3. the word in which the long *e* sound is spelled *ei:* _____

4. the word that ends with a *z:* _____

5. the word that contains a double vowel: _____

EXERCISE B

On the lines provided, write the spelling words that contain the same letters as the corresponding smaller words.

1. full _____   **6.** end _____

2. own _____   **7.** pun _____

3. quart _____   **8.** it _____

4. eat _____   **9.** port _____

5. rim _____   **10.** half _____

EXERCISE C

Study the letters underlined in each word. On the lines provided, write the spelling words with the same letter patterns.

1. dec<u>ei</u>ve _____   **6.** ram<u>bl</u>ing _____

2. <u>off</u>er _____   **7.** ni<u>ck</u>name _____

3. a<u>cr</u>imony _____   **8.** ar<u>t</u>ery _____

4. de<u>f</u>iant _____   **9.** mis<u>pl</u>ace _____

5. relea<u>s</u>ed _____   **10.** <u>t</u>ournament _____

DECODING WORKSHEET

User Friendly
T. Ernesto Bethancourt

Pupil's Edition page 356

Long and Short Vowel Sounds

Thinking about these spelling patterns can often help you decide if vowel sounds are long or short when you are decoding unfamiliar words.

- The VC + *e* (vowel, consonant + *e*) pattern is a clue that the vowel sound is long, as in *code*
- The VCCV (vowel, consonant, consonant, vowel) pattern in a two-syllable word is a clue that the first vowel is short, as in *summit*
- The VCV (vowel, consonant, vowel) pattern in a two-syllable word is a clue that the first vowel is long, as in *vapor*

EXERCISE A

Read the words listed below. Decide if the vowel sound in each underlined syllable is long or short, and draw a circle around your answer. Then, on the line provided, write the letter pattern that was your clue.

EXAMPLE: butter	but ter	long or (short)	_VCCV_
1. hypnotize	hyp no tize	long or short	_____
2. slippers	slip pers	long or short	_____
3. pantomime	pan to mime	long or short	_____
4. million	mil lion	long or short	_____
5. percussion	per cus sion	long or short	_____
6. notice	no tice	long or short	_____
7. mansion	man sion	long or short	_____
8. fabricate	fab ri cate	long or short	_____
9. console	con sole	long or short	_____
10. message	mes sage	long or short	_____

EXERCISE B

The words *local* and *locker* both begin with *loc*, but in *local* the first vowel sound is long, and in *locker* the first vowel sound is short. In each of the words below, the first vowel sound is long. On each line provided, write a word that begins with the same three letters but has a short vowel sound in the first syllable.

EXAMPLE: patron _____*pattern*_____

1. pilot _____
2. baby _____
3. diner _____
4. minor _____
5. super _____

SPELLING WORKSHEET

Miss Awful
Arthur Cavanaugh

Pupil's Edition page 368

Spelling Homonyms

The words below illustrate the complexity of the English language. Homonyms are words that sound the same but have different (sometimes very different) spellings and meanings. Study this group of homonyms. (At least one word in each pair is from "Miss Awful.")

eight/ate	hours/ours	one/won	sense/cents	wait/weight
flower/flour	lesson/lessen	reign/rain	stairs/stares	waste/waist
him/hymn	nose/knows	roll/role	steal/steel	week/weak

EXERCISE A

On the lines provided, write the pairs of spelling words that match each pronunciation.

1. sterz _____

2. wāst _____

3. nōz _____

4. les′ən _____

5. wāt _____

6. ᴏᴜrz _____

7. āt _____

8. stēl _____

9. wēk _____

10. rān _____

EXERCISE B

On the lines provided, write the missing consonants that complete each pair of spelling words.

1. __ __ ea __ / __ __ ee __

2. __ i __ / __ y __ __

3. __ o __ __ / __ o __ e

4. __ __ o __ e __ / __ __ ou __

5. o __ e / __ o __

6. __ ai __ / __ ei __ __ __

7. __ e __ __ e / __ e __ __ __

8. __ ee __ / __ ea __

9. __ ei __ __ / __ ai __

10. __ e __ __ o __ / __ e __ __ e __

EXERCISE C

On the lines provided, write the spelling words that match each of the following definitions.

1. take away secretly/a hard metal: _____ / _____

2. use up without real need/part of the body between the ribs and hips:

    _____ / _____

3. masculine pronoun/a song of praise: _____ / _____

4. a blossom/a fine substance produced by grinding grain: _____ / _____

5. a single unit/finished in first place: _____ / _____

SPELLING WORKSHEET

Sky Woman
retold by Joseph Bruchac

Pupil's Edition page 426

✔ **How to Own a Word**
Adding Suffixes: Change _y_ to _i_

On the lines provided, write the new words formed by adding the suffix in parentheses to each of the following words.

1. easy (-er) _____

2. happy (-ly) _____

3. pretty (-er) _____

4. lonely (-ness) _____

5. stormy (-est) _____

6. weary (-some) _____

Adding Suffixes to Words that End in _y_

When words end in _y_ preceded by a consonant, change the _y_ to _i_ before any suffix that does not begin with _i_. These suffixes include -_ed_, -_ful_, -_es_, -_er_, -_est_, and -_ness_. For example, _cry_ plus the suffix -_ed_ becomes _cried_, and _hurry_ plus the suffix -_es_ becomes _hurries_. Of course, there are always exceptions. For example, when you add the suffix -_ness_ or -_ly_ to a word, you don't always change the spelling of the word itself. As a result _sly_ plus -_ly_ becomes _slyly_. When a suffix begins with _i_, simply add it to the end of the word. For example, _cry_ plus the suffix -_ing_ becomes _crying_. Practice adding suffixes to these spelling words from "Sky Woman."

belly	bury	muddy	story
berry	marry	sky	try

EXERCISE A

On the lines provided, add the suffix indicated in parentheses to each of the spelling words.

1. sky (-es) _____

2. berry (-es) _____

3. try (-ing) _____

4. belly (-es) _____

5. story (-es) _____

6. bury (-ing) _____

7. muddy (-est) _____

8. marry (-ed) _____

EXERCISE B

Fill in the lines provided with the appropriate variation of the spelling words.

EXAMPLE: "Sky Woman" is one of many creation _____ _stories_ . _(story)_

1. The Good Mind made _____ of all kinds. _(berry)_

2. Flint _____ the water and made it foul-smelling. _(muddy)_

3. The chief of the Sky World _____ a young woman. _(marry)_

4. With the help of Sky Woman, the Good Mind _____ his mother. _(bury)_

5. Sky Woman _____ to warn her daughter not to go west. _(try)_

Elements of Literature

NAME _____ CLASS _____ DATE _____

When the Earth Shakes
Patricia Lauber   **Pupil's Edition page 434**

Spelling Vivid Verbs

The verbs in "When the Earth Shakes" are so vivid that they almost grab and shake you. What gives them such power? Perhaps it's the letter patterns that imitate each sound or sensation as you say the word. Can you feel the rumbling and shaking in *tremble*? Study the letter patterns that make the following words so effective.

bounced	cracked	plunged	shuddered	trembled
buckled	flooded	roared	snapped	triggered
clawed	jolted	shook	swept	twisted

EXERCISE A

On the lines provided, write the spelling words that make the same sound as the underlined letters in each of the following words.

1. practi<u>ce</u> _____

2. h<u>u</u>ngry _____

3. bi<u>gg</u>er _____

4. r<u>ou</u>nd _____

5. underst<u>oo</u>d _____

6. confi<u>sc</u>ated _____

7. consi<u>d</u>ered _____

8. br<u>ough</u>t _____

9. f<u>oa</u>ming _____

10. p<u>or</u>tray _____

EXERCISE B

On the lines provided, write the spelling words that contain the same letters as the corresponding smaller words.

1. lunge _____

2. awe _____

3. is _____

4. nap _____

5. ounce _____

6. ode _____

7. rig _____

8. hook _____

9. oar _____

10. rack _____

EXERCISE C

In the boxes provided, write the spelling words whose letters match each shape.

1.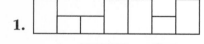

2.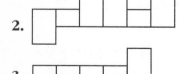

3.

4.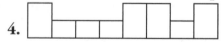

5.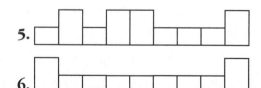

6.

Elements of Literature

DECODING WORKSHEET

from Survive the Savage Sea
Dougal Robertson

Consonant Combinations

When you need to decode words with strange combinations of consonants, remember these strategies:

- Look for consonant pairs *ch, sh, th,* and *wh.* Remember that these letter pairs stand for just one sound when they are in the same syllable.
- Analyze the word. If the word is a compound word, divide it into its parts. If it has prefixes, suffixes, or inflectional endings, pull those off and take a look at what's left.
- Consider the possibility that a letter might be silent. If it's hard to include a letter sound or if the word sounds strange when you do, there's a good chance the problem letter is a silent letter.
- Remember that the letter *w* is not always a consonant. It can be part of the spelling of a vowel sound (as in *how, draw,* and *stew*).

EXERCISE A

On each line provided, write one of the words listed below next to the consonant combination that appears in it.

seamanship	knowing	landscape	hymn
wrinkled	thought	dinghy	acknowledgment
awkward	shark	crawled	anxious

1. ght _____

2. rk _____

3. nkl _____

4. ckn _____

5. nsh _____

6. wkw _____

7. ndsc _____

8. ngh _____

9. nx _____

10. mn _____

EXERCISE B

Write the word or words from Exercise A that match each description.

1. the four words in which *w* is part of the spelling of a vowel sound

_____, _____, _____, _____

2. the word in which the *n* is silent _____

3. the two words in which *sh* stands for just one sound _____,

_____

4. the four words in which *w* precedes a consonant _____,

_____, _____, _____

5. the word in which /sh/ is spelled *xi* _____

Elements of Literature

SPELLING WORKSHEET

Antaeus
Borden Deal

Spelling Contractions Correctly

A contraction is a shortened form of a word or group of words. The apostrophe in a contraction indicates where a letter or letters have been left out. The word *not* is shortened to *n't, is* or *has* is shortened to *'s, will* is shortened to *'ll, would* or *had* is shortened to *'d,* and *are* is shortened to *'re.* Usually, you can just add the contracted word to another word without changing the other word's spelling, but sometimes the other word's spelling is changed. For example, the contraction *won't* is a combination of the words *will* and *not.* Practice spelling these contractions from "Antaeus."

can't	he'd	it's	wasn't	won't
didn't	I'd	that's	we'll	wouldn't
don't	I'll	there's	what's	you're

EXERCISE A

On the lines provided, add the missing consonants to the following contractions.

1. ____ e'____

2. ____ ____ e ____ e'____

3. ____ e'____ ____

4. ____ a ____ ____'____

5. I'____ ____

6. ____ ou'____ e

7. i ____'____

8. ____ i ____ ____'____

9. ____ a ____'____

10. ____ ou ____ ____ ____'____

EXERCISE B

On the lines provided, classify the contractions from the list above by the words they have in common. Two contractions should appear twice.

would / had	not	is / has
1. _____	**7.** _____	**13.** _____
2. _____	**8.** _____	**14.** _____
3. _____	**9.** _____	**15.** _____
	10. _____	**16.** _____
will	**11.** _____	
4. _____	**12.** _____	are
5. _____		**17.** _____
6. _____		

SPELLING WORKSHEET

The Origin of the Seasons
retold by Olivia Coolidge

Pupil's Edition page 500

✔ How to Own a Word: Prefixes

Add the following prefixes to root words in order to form new words. Write the new words on the lines provided.

1. anti- _____

2. auto- _____

3. hydro- _____

4. meta- _____

5. sym- *or* syn- _____

Spelling Words from Mythology

From earliest times, people have used myths to explain unanswered questions. Many of the words used in myths are still part of our vocabulary today. The words below are from "The Origin of the Seasons."

ambrosia	goddess	hero	majestic	palace
chariot	harvest	lyre	mighty	pomegranate
dignity	messenger	immortal	Olympus	underworld

EXERCISE A

On the lines provided, write the spelling words that match each of the pronunciations.

1. mīt′ē _____

2. hir′ō _____

3. char′ē•ət _____

4. līr _____

5. ō•lim′pəs _____

6. här′vist _____

7. gäd′is _____

8. mə•jes′tik _____

9. un′dər•wʉrld′ _____

10. päm′ə•gran′•it _____

EXERCISE B

Fill in the lines provided with the consonants that are missing from the following spelling words.

1. ____ i ____ ____ i ____ y

2. ____ a ____ a ____ e

3. i ____ ____ o ____ ____ a ____

4. a ____ ____ ____ o ____ ia

5. ____ i ____ ____ ____ y

6. ____ e ____ ____ e ____ ____ e ____

7. u ____ ____ e ____ ____ o ____ ____ ____

8. ____ ____ a ____ io ____

9. ____ e ____ o

10. ____ a ____ e ____ ____ i ____

Elements of Literature

Spelling and Decoding Worksheets **23**

SPELLING WORKSHEET

Orpheus, the Great Musician
retold by Olivia Coolidge   **Pupil's Edition page 512**

Spelling Words Containing Inflected Endings −s, −ed, −ing

English is an *inflected* language, which means that as a verb's uses change, its spelling also changes. That is why we say *I smile* but *he smiles.* We show time changes with she *smiled* and she *was smiling.* These guidelines for adding suffixes will help you to spell inflected forms correctly.

1. Drop a final silent *e* before a suffix beginning with a vowel (such as *-ed* or *-ing*).
2. Double the final consonant before a suffix beginning with a vowel *if* the word has only one syllable and ends in a single consonant preceded by a single vowel.
3. Do not double the final consonant before a suffix beginning with a vowel.

Study these words from "Orpheus, the Great Musician."

ascended	deceiving	hastened	stopped	taking
ceased	dissolved	passed	stretched	thinned
crossing	flitting	rejoiced	stumbled	yawning

EXERCISE A

On the lines provided, write each spelling word under the heading for the guideline you must follow to add a suffix to the word. You may need to use a dictionary for this exercise.

Guideline 1   **Guideline 2**

1. _____   7. _____   12. _____

2. _____   8. _____   13. _____

3. _____   9. _____   14. _____

4. _____   **Guideline 3**   15. _____

5. _____   10. _____

6. _____   11. _____

EXERCISE B

Study the underlined letters in these words. On the lines provided, write the spelling words that contain the same letter patterns.

1. inv**oic**ed _____   6. crumb**ling** _____

2. w**as**ted _____   7. di**s**appear _____

3. displ**eas**ing _____   8. inno**c**ent _____

4. br**eak**ing _____   9. per**ceiv**ed _____

5. r**os**iness _____   10. pet**tin**ess _____

DECODING WORKSHEET

Echo and Narcissus
retold by Roger Lancelyn Green   **Pupil's Edition page 522**

Reading Greek Words

When reading words that come from Greek, including the names of characters in Greek myths, remember the following things:

• The letter *y* usually stands for short *i*, as it does in *myth*.
• Greek words usually have as many syllables as they have vowels.
• The letters *eu* sometimes stand for one vowel sound, /oo/ as in *zoo*, and sometimes stand for two vowel sounds, long *e* and the unstressed vowel sound schwa, as in *Orpheus* (ôr´ fē əs).

EXERCISE A

Read these names of people and places from Greek mythology.

Styx	Echo	Aphrodite
Olympus	Charon	Arachne
Persephone	Elysium	Lydia

1. Write the name that sounds like *sticks*. _____

2. Write the two names in which *ph* stands for /f/. _____, _____

3. Write the name that begins with long *o*. _____

4. Write the names in which *y* stands for short *i* and *i* stands for long *e*. _____, _____

5. Write the three names in which *ch* stands for /k/. _____, _____, _____

EXERCISE B

Read these names from Greek mythology.

Eurydice   Odysseus   Eurystheus   Orpheus   Europa   Zeus

1. Write the four names in which *eu* stands for one vowel sound. _____, _____, _____, _____

2. Write the three names in which *eu* stands for two vowel sounds. _____, _____, _____

3. Which name did you write twice? _____

4. Write the three names that have four syllables. _____, _____, _____

5. Write the two names that have three syllables. _____, _____

Elements of Literature   *Spelling and Decoding Worksheets* **25**

NAME _____ CLASS _____ DATE _____

SPELLING WORKSHEET

The Labors of Hercules
retold by Rex Warner   **Pupil's Edition page 540**

Spelling Words That Are Often Misspelled

Below is a list of words from "The Labors of Hercules." Each word has a special characteristic that may make it difficult to spell: double letters, silent letters, words that are not spelled the way they are pronounced, and so on. It might help to divide the multisyllabic words into separate syllables in order to make their spellings easier to remember.

accomplished	difficult	guardian	recognize	though
actually	experience	heights	source	through
approached	explanation	jealous	successful	wholly

EXERCISE A Complete this crossword grid with the spelling words.

Copyright © by Holt, Rinehart and Winston. All rights reserved.

EXERCISE B

On the lines provided, write the spelling words that match each of the following descriptions.

1. six words with double consonants: _____ , _____ ,

_____ , _____ , _____ , _____

2. three words in which the sound /ō/ is spelled differently:

_____ , _____ , _____

3. two words in which *ough* has different sounds: _____ ,

_____

4. six words in which the *e* is silent (not limited to the ends of words):

_____ , _____ , _____ ,

_____ , _____

5. three words in which the sound /s/ is spelled *c:* _____ ,

_____ , _____

DECODING WORKSHEET

Aschenputtel, retold by Jakob and Wilhelm Grimm
translated by Lucy Crane   **Pupil's Edition page 592**

Spelling Words with Germanic Roots

We inherited the words listed below from Old English, a Germanic language with many words borrowed from Scandinavian languages. Study the following spelling words.

belong	evening	follow	maiden
clothes	evil	heaven	thank
daughter	fetch	laugh	wedding

EXERCISE A

On the lines provided, write the spelling words that are derived from each of the following Old English words. You may need to use a dictionary.

1. fetian _____
2. clathas _____
3. æfnung _____
4. heofon _____
5. mægden _____
6. yfel _____

7. thancian _____
8. langian _____
9. folgian _____
10. weddung _____
11. dohtor _____
12. hleahhan _____

EXERCISE B

On the lines provided, write the spelling words that contain the same letters as the corresponding smaller words.

1. low _____
2. clot _____
3. heave _____
4. aught _____
5. an _____

6. din _____
7. etch _____
8. aid _____
9. eve _____
10. long _____

EXERCISE C

On the lines provided, write the spelling words that match each description.

1. the word in which the sound /z/ is spelled *es:* _____
2. the word in which the sound /f/ is spelled *gh:* _____
3. the word in which the *t* is silent: _____
4. the word in which the sound /ā/ is spelled *ai:* _____
5. the word in which the sound /ô/ is spelled *augh:* _____

SPELLING WORKSHEET

The Algonquin Cinderella, retold by M. R. Cox
Yeh-Shen, retold by Ai-Ling Louie

Pupil's Edition page 607

✔ **How to Own a Word: Doubling Consonants Before Suffixes**

On the lines provided, use the rules for doubling consonants before suffixes to write each word correctly.

1. slip + -er _____

2. order + -ed _____

3. bid + -ing _____

4. begin + -er _____

5. rag + -ed _____

6. remain + -ing _____

7. run + -er _____

8. sad + -en _____

9. happen + -ing _____

10. drop + -ed _____

Spelling Words Ending in *e* and *y*

The spelling words listed below all end in *e* or *y*. Exercises A and B focus on adding suffixes to these spelling words. Use the guidelines that follow to help you learn the spelling of these words.

aware (–ness)	day (–ly)	harmony (–ize)	lively (–ness)
beauty (–ful)	desire (–ous)	heavy (–ly)	lonely (–ness)
crafty (–ness)	fine (–ery)	hungry (–er)	wide (–en)

1. Drop a final silent *e* before a suffix beginning with a vowel. For example, *approve + al* becomes *approval.*

2. Keep a final silent *e* before a suffix beginning with a consonant. For example, *love + ly* becomes *lovely.*

3. Change a final *y* to *i* before a suffix beginning with a consonant. For example, *easy + ly* becomes *easily.*

4. Remember, there are many exceptions to these guidelines.

EXERCISE A

Study the suffixes in parentheses listed above. Add each one to the word it follows. Write the new words on the lines provided.

1. aware _____

2. beauty _____

3. crafty _____

4. day _____

5. desire _____

6. fine _____

7. harmony _____

8. heavy _____

9. hungry _____

10. lively _____

11. lonely _____

12. wide _____

EXERCISE B

Study the new words you made in Exercise A. Next to each new word, write the number of the guideline you used to create it.

SPELLING WORKSHEET

Oni and the Great Bird
retold by Abayomi Fuja   **Pupil's Edition page 628**

Words with *ie*

Together, the letters *ie* are pronounced in different ways. Notice the different ways these letters are pronounced in words from "Oni and the Great Bird."

- *ie* stands for short *i* in *friend*
- *ie* stands for long *e* in *pieces*
- *ie* stands for two sounds—long *i* and the unstressed sound schwa—in *quiet*
- *ie* stands for two other sounds—long *e* and schwa—in *audience*

EXERCISE A

Read these words. Write each word under the key word—*friend, pieces, quiet,* or *audience*—in which *ie* stands for the same sound or sounds.

brief	diet	twentieth	furrier	client
science	siege	obedient	mischief	experience

friend   **pieces**

1. _____   2. _____

                                            3. _____

quiet   **audience**

4. _____   7. _____

5. _____   8. _____

6. _____   9. _____

                                            10. _____

EXERCISE B

Read each of these words. Show that you know how *ie* is pronounced in each word by writing a rhyming word that does not contain the *ie* letter combination.

1. friend _____   **6.** spiel _____

2. tried _____   **7.** frieze _____

3. view _____   **8.** flier _____

4. diesel _____   **9.** fief _____

5. eerie _____   **10.** shield _____

SPELLING WORKSHEET

Master Frog
retold by Lynette Dyer Vuong Pupil's Edition page 638

Spelling Multisyllabic Words

Many multisyllabic words look difficult to spell because they have so many letters. However, if you separate these long words into separate syllables and focus on one syllable at a time, spelling the words is much easier. Try this strategy with the following words from "Master Frog."

accompanied	astonishment	entreaties	intelligence	presumptuous
admonished	contemptuous	fascinated	mischievous	prosperity
affectionate	destiny	genuinely	mysterious	transformation

EXERCISE A

Separate each of the following spelling words into syllables, and write the syllables on the lines provided. Use dashes to mark breaks between syllables. You may need to use a dictionary to identify where one syllable ends and another begins.

1. admonished _____
2. affectionate _____
3. astonishment _____
4. contemptuous _____
5. intelligence _____

6. mischievous _____
7. mysterious _____
8. presumptuous _____
9. prosperity _____
10. transformation _____

EXERCISE B

On the lines provided, write the spelling words that match each pronunciation.

1. ə•fek′shən•it _____
2. prē•zump′chōō•əs _____
3. mis′chə•vəs _____
4. jen′yōō•in•lē _____
5. en•trēt′ēz _____

6. fas′ə•nāt′•əd _____
7. ə•kum′pə•nēd _____
8. mis•tir′ē•əs _____
9. kən•temp′chōō•əs _____
10. des′tə•nē _____

EXERCISE C

On the lines provided, write the correct spelling of each misspelled word.

1. mischevious _____
2. fasinated _____
3. contemptous _____
4. prizumshus _____
5. intreties _____

6. afectionate _____
7. misterius _____
8. genunely _____
9. inteligens _____
10. destiney _____

30 *Spelling and Decoding Worksheets* *Elements of Literature*

SPELLING WORKSHEET

Sealskin, Soulskin
retold by Clarissa Pinkola Estés   **Pupil's Edition page 649**

Spelling Inuit Words and Words of the Far North

These words are part of the way of life of the Inuit, a culture rich in Arctic wisdom and lore. Practice spelling these words from "Sealskin, Soulskin."

freeze	mukluks (boots)	salmon	whale
ice floes	otters	sealskins	whiskers
kayak	parka	walrus	winter

EXERCISE A

In the boxes provided, write the spelling words whose letters match each shape.

1.

6.

2.

7.

3.

8.

4.

9.

5.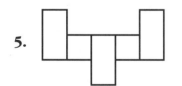

10.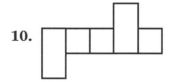

EXERCISE B

Unscramble each of these spelling words, and write the correctly spelled words on the lines provided.

1. lursaw _____

2. zefere _____

3. twiner _____

4. storet _____

5. yakak _____

6. noslam _____

7. ehlaw _____

8. slicefoe _____

9. srekwish _____

10. slakesins _____

Collection One: Out Here on My Own

Rikki-tikki-tavi, page 1

Exercise A

1. most careful
2. more dangerous
3. angrier
4. most sorrowfully
5. nearest

Exercise B

1. earliest
2. safer
3. wiser
4. sooner
5. faintest

Song of the Trees, page 2

Exercise A

1. incredulously
2. suspiciously
3. already, nearby
4. comfortably, curtly
5. here

Exercise B

1. nearby
2. down
3. comfortably
4. haughtily
5. gently
6. afterward
7. enough
8. away
9. softly
10. later

The Smallest Dragonboy, page 3

Exercise A

1. glorious
2. constriction
3. resentful
4. traditional
5. opportunity

Exercise B

1. opportunity
2. argument
3. resentful
4. swiftness
5. constriction
6. flexible

7. unmistakable
8. harmless

Three Skeleton Key, page 4

Exercise A

(Order of responses for 1–3; 4–8; and 9–15 will vary.)

1. coast guard
2. patrol boat
3. no one
4. glassed-in
5. knee-deep
6. old-timers
7. twenty-four
8. well-placed
9. footfall
10. lighthouse
11. metalwork
12. nightfall
13. stronghold
14. sundown
15. windmill

Exercise B

1. patrol boat
2. glassed-in
3. footfall
4. windmill
5. metalwork
6. lighthouse
7. sundown
8. twenty-four
9. nightfall
10. knee-deep
11. no one
12. coast guard
13. old-timers
14. well-placed
15. stronghold

A Day's Wait, page 5

Exercise A

1. ptomaine
2. psychology
3. pneumonia
4. pseudonym
5. pterodactyl
6. pterodactyl
7. psychology
8. ptomaine
9. pseudonym
10. pneumonia

Exercise B

1. emphasis
2. graphic
3. phonics
4. phantom
5. physician

6. emphasis
7. phantom
8. phonics
9. graphic
10. physician

Collection Two: Who Am I?

from *Homesick,* page 6

Exercise A

1. straight
2. truly
3. dreamed
4. crooked
5. please
6. classes

Exercise B

1. gradually
2. clutched
3. freedom
4. broad-brimmed
5. truly
6. flustered
7. straight
8. glowering
9. probably
10. o'clock

Exercise C

1. please
2. flustered
3. interest
4. gradually
5. broad-brimmed
6. glowering
7. crooked
8. freedom
9. probably
10. classes

from *Barrio Boy,* page 7

Exercise A

1. patiently
2. attention
3. blackboard
4. principal
5. knowledge
6. recitations
7. interpreter
8. enrolling
9. announcements
10. friendliness

Exercise B

1. announcements, attention, enrolling, friendliness, progress

2. attention, consultations, patiently, recitations
3. announcements, pronounce
4. consultations, formidable, graduated, interpreter, recitations
5. knowledge

Fish Cheeks, page 8

Exercise A

1. cod
2. fungus
3. polite
4. appreciate
5. tofu
6. menu
7. platters
8. squid
9. turkey
10. prawns

Exercise B

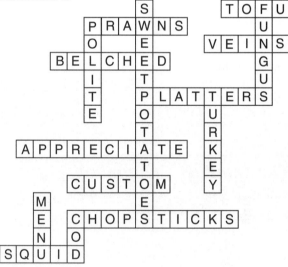

Names / Nombres, page 9

Exercise A

(Responses may vary somewhat. Accept all reasonable responses.)

1. im mi grate   im mi gra tion
2. cel e brate   cel e bra tion
3. dis trib ute   dis tri bu tion
4. ex plain   ex pla na tion

5. (mul) ti ply   mul ti pli (ca) tion
6. de (fine)   def i (ni) tion
7. par (tic) i pate   par tic i (pa) tion
8. (lim) it   lim i (ta) tion
9. re (sign)   res ig (na) tion
10. (dic) tate   dic (ta) tion

Exercise B

1. 4   communication   5
2. 2   revision   3
3. 2   declaration   4
4. 3   population   4
5. 2   reservation   4

The Naming of Names, page 10

Exercise A

1. submerged
2. encyclopedia

3. insane
4. perspire
5. atmosphere
6. constructing
7. anachronism
8. philosophy
9. quietly
10. sensible

Exercise B

1. dissolve
2. precise
3. insane
4. convivial
5. submerged
6. constructing
7. altitude
8. archaeologist

Collection Three: Do the Right Thing

After Twenty Years, page 11

Exercise A

1. cigar, egotism
2. certain, cigar
3. correspond, compete
4. pacific, success
5. passengers, submerged

Exercise B

(Order of responses for 1–2; 3–4; 5–6; and 7–8 will vary.)

1. panic
2. description
3. existence
4. announced
5. swagger
6. eager
7. dangerous
8. stranger

A Mason-Dixon Memory, page 12

Exercise A

1. boxes
2. knives
3. radios
4. comedies
5. scientists
6. monkeys
7. birches
8. photos
9. chairwomen
10. arrangements
11. churches

12. bushes
13. dresses
14. trophies
15. theories

Exercise B

1. parishes
2. lives
3. speeches
4. statues
5. boundaries
6. attorneys
7. disasters
8. coaches
9. ladies
10. friendships

The No-Guitar Blues, page 13

✔ **How to Own a Word**

1. C
2. received
3. achieved
4. eerie
5. priest

Exercise A

1. license
2. brighter
3. pleasant
4. watched
5. sweat
6. through
7. weird
8. earn

9. deceitful
10. special

Exercise B

1. pleasant
2. through
3. perpetual
4. brighter
5. scratch
6. sweat
7. caught
8. heard
9. license
10. guitar

Bargain, page 14

✔ **How to Own a Word**

1. climbed
2. C
3. consigned
4. hustle
5. pneumonia

Exercise A

1. boardwalk, buckboard, overshoes, pitchfork
2. harness shop, saddle horse, whiskey barrel
3. saloon

4. blizzard
5. buttes

Exercise B

1. mercantile
2. lantern
3. moustache
4. freighter
5. blizzard

Amigo Brothers, page 15

Exercise A

1. stillness
2. immediately
3. community
4. challenger
5. medallion
6. announcer
7. bragging
8. corridor
9. flurry
10. surrounding

Exercise B

1. flurry
2. medallion
3. progress
4. corridor
5. profession
6. announcer
7. dispelled
8. occasionally
9. surrounding
10. approval

Exercise C

1. dispelled
2. corridor
3. medallion
4. community
5. profession

Collection Four: We Rookies Have to Stick Together

Brian's Song, page 16

Exercise A

1. cleats
2. end zone
3. receiver
4. blitz
5. playbook

Exercise B

1. fullback
2. touchdown
3. quarterback
4. cleats
5. scrimmage
6. end zone

7. punt
8. blitz
9. sportscaster
10. halfback

Exercise C

1. receiver
2. offense
3. scrimmage
4. defense
5. cleats
6. blitz
7. kickoff
8. quarterback
9. playbook
10. touchdown

Collection Five: Living in the Heart

User Friendly, page 17

Exercise A

1. long   VC + e
2. short   VCCV

3. long   VC + e
4. short   VCCV
5. short   VCCV
6. long   VCV
7. short   VCCV

8. short   VCCV
9. long   VC + e
10. short   VCCV

Exercise B

(Answers will vary. Sample responses follow.)

1. pillow
2. babble
3. dinner
4. minnow
5. supple

Miss Awful, page 18

Exercise A

1. stairs/stares   2. waste/waist

3. nose/knows
4. lesson/lessen
5. wait/weight
6. hours/ours
7. eight/ate
8. steal/steel
9. week/weak
10. reign/rain

Exercise B

1. steal/steel
2. him/hymn
3. roll/role
4. flower/flour
5. one/won
6. wait/weight
7. sense/cents
8. week/weak
9. reign/rain
10. lesson/lessen

Exercise C

1. steal/steel
2. waste/waist
3. him/hymn
4. flower/flour
5. one/won

Collection Six: This Old Earth

Sky Woman, page 19

✔ **How to Own a Word**

1. easier
2. happily
3. prettier
4. loneliness
5. stormiest
6. wearisome

Exercise A

1. skies
2. berries
3. trying
4. bellies
5. stories
6. burying
7. muddiest
8. married

Exercise B

1. berries
2. muddied
3. married (*or* marries)
4. buried (*or* buries)
5. tried (*or* tries)

When the Earth Shakes, page 20

Exercise A

(Some items have more than one possible answer.)

1. cracked
2. plunged
3. triggered
4. bounced
5. shook
6. twisted
7. shuddered
8. clawed
9. jolted
10. roared

Exercise B

1. plunged
2. clawed
3. twisted
4. snapped
5. bounced
6. flooded
7. triggered
8. shook
9. roared
10. cracked

Exercise C

1. buckled
2. jolted
3. swept
4. trembled
5. shuddered
6. triggered

---

from *Survive the Savage Sea,* page 21

Exercise A

1. thought
2. shark
3. wrinkled
4. acknowledgment
5. seamanship
6. awkward
7. landscape
8. dinghy
9. anxious
10. hymn

Exercise B

1. awkward, knowing, acknowledgment, crawled
2. hymn
3. seamanship, shark
4. wrinkled, awkward, acknowledgment, crawled
5. anxious

Antaeus, page 22

Exercise A

1. he'd
2. there's
3. we'll
4. wasn't
5. I'll
6. you're
7. it's
8. didn't
9. can't
10. wouldn't

Exercise B

(Order of responses for 1-3; 4-6; 7-12; and 13-16 will vary.)

1. he'd
2. I'd
3. wouldn't
4. I'll
5. we'll
6. won't

Elements of Literature

Spelling and Decoding Worksheets: Answer Key **37**

Copyright © by Holt, Rinehart and Winston. All rights reserved.

ANSWER KEY

7. can't	10. wasn't	13. it's	16. what's
8. didn't	11. won't	14. that's	17. you're
9. don't	12. wouldn't	15. there's	

Collection Seven: Our Classical Heritage

The Origin of the Seasons, page 23

✔ How to Own a Word

(Answers will vary. Sample answers follow.)

1. antibiotic
2. automobile
3. hydroelectric
4. metaphor
5. sympathy; synonym

Exercise A

1. mighty
2. hero
3. chariot
4. lyre
5. Olympus
6. harvest
7. goddess
8. majestic
9. underworld
10. pomegranate

Exercise B

1. dignity
2. palace
3. immortal
4. ambrosia
5. mighty
6. messenger
7. underworld
8. chariot
9. hero
10. majestic

Orpheus, the Great Musician, page 24

Exercise A

(Order of responses for 1–6; 7–9; and 10–15 will vary.)

1. ceased
2. deceiving
3. dissolved
4. rejoiced
5. stumbled
6. taking
7. flitting
8. stopped
9. thinned
10. ascended
11. crossing
12. hastened
13. passed
14. stretched
15. yawning

Exercise B

1. rejoiced
2. hastened
3. ceased
4. taking

5. crossing
6. stumbled
7. dissolved
8. thinned
9. deceiving
10. flitting

Echo and Narcissus, page 25

Exercise A

1. Styx
2. Persephone, Aphrodite
3. Olympus
4. Elysium, Lydia
5. Echo, Charon, Arachne

Exercise B

1. Eurydice, Eurystheus, Europa, Zeus
2. Odysseus, Eurystheus, Orpheus
3. Eurystheus
4. Eurydice, Odysseus, Eurystheus
5. Orpheus, Europa

The Labors of Hercules, page 26

Exercise A

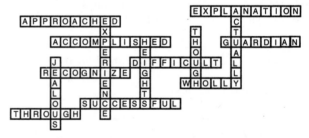

Exercise B

1. accomplished, actually, approached, difficult, successful, wholly
2. approached, though, wholly
3. though, through
4. accomplished, approached, experience, heights, recognize, source
5. experience, successful, source

Collection Eight: 900 Cinderellas: Our World Heritage in Folklore

Aschenputtel, page 27

Exercise A

1. fetched
2. clothes
3. evening
4. heaven
5. maiden
6. evil
7. thanked
8. belonged
9. followed
10. wedding
11. daughter
12. laughing

Exercise B

1. followed	6. wedding
2. clothes	7. fetched
3. heaven	8. maiden
4. daughter	9. evening
5. thanked	10. belonged

Exercise C

1. clothes	4. maiden
2. laughing	5. daughter
3. fetched	

The Algonquin Cinderella / Yeh-Shen, page 28

✔ How to Own a Word

1. slipper	6. remaining
2. ordered	7. runner
3. bidding	8. sadden
4. beginner	9. happening
5. ragged	10. dropped

Exercises A and B

1. awareness—2	7. harmonize—4
2. beautiful—3	8. heavily—3
3. craftiness—3	9. hungrier—4
4. daily—3	10. liveliness—3
5. desirous—1	11. loneliness—3
6. finery—1	12. widen—1

Oni and the Great Bird, page 29

Exercise A

(Order of responses for 2-3; 4-6; and 7-10 will vary.)

1. mischief	6. client
2. brief	7. twentieth
3. siege	8. obedient
4. science	9. furrier
5. diet	10. experience

Exercise B

(Answers will vary. Sample responses follow.)

1. spend	6. real
2. ride	7. breeze
3. new	8. tire
4. weasel	9. leaf
5. weary	10. peeled

Master Frog, page 30

Exercise A

1. ad—mon—ished	
2. af—fec—tion—ate	
3. as—ton—ish—ment	
4. con—temp—tu—ous	
5. in—tel—li—gence	
6. mis—chie—vous	
7. mys—te—ri—ous	
8. pre—sump—tu—ous	
9. pros—per—i—ty	
10. trans—for—ma—tion	

Exercise B

1. affectionate	6. fascinated
2. presumptuous	7. accompanied
3. mischievous	8. mysterious
4. genuinely	9. contemptuous
5. entreaties	10. destiny

Exercise C

1. mischievous	6. affectionate
2. fascinated	7. mysterious
3. contemptuous	8. genuinely
4. presumptuous	9. intelligence
5. entreaties	10. destiny

Sealskin, Soulskin, page 31

Exercise A

1. freeze	6. whiskers
2. sealskins	7. mukluks
3. walrus *or* salmon	8. otters
4. winter	9. whale
5. kayak	10. parka

Exercise B

1. walrus	6. salmon
2. freeze	7. whale
3. winter	8. ice floes
4. otters	9. whiskers
5. kayak	10. sealskins